Leonardo da Vinci

ABBEY LIBRARY
LONDON

Leonard

o da Vinci

Translated from Romanian as published by
MERIDIANE PUBLISHING HOUSE
Bucharest, 1978
under the original title of
LEONARDO DA VINCI

Introductory study, anthology of texts,
selection of illustrations
and chronology by
VICTOR IERONIM STOICHIŢĂ

Translated into English by
ANDREEA GHEORGHIŢOIU

LEONARDO TO-DAY

More than four centuries and a half after Leonardo's death, when the Campbell can of soup concentrate has triumphantly entered exhibitions and museums and the moustaches once painted on the portrait of Mona Lisa are an unavoidable event in the art history of our century, an album with colour reproductions of Leonardo's work becomes a manifestation — be it ever so modest — of the vitality of his artistic creation, a solemn peak which has long since pierced the thickest, the highest, the most recalcitrant layer of clouds.

Indeed, what has changed in the 450 years that have elapsed since Leonardo's death is not his work — apart from the gradual dimming of The Last Supper *in Milan — but the manner in which we can approach it today.*

It is unquestionable that Leonardo belongs to the history of the human mind. That is why today any attempt at approaching his work can be neither commendatory nor disparaging; on the contrary, it must, at any cost, ascertain facts at least, it must be as lucid and true as possible.

It is common knowledge that he produced few paintings. Some of the most reliable specialists held that the scientific genius surpassed the artist. Leonardo himself believed that his art was science. So can we hold that the scientific genius was greater? Vasari describes him as a belated penitent on his death bed. What he says deserves to be quoted in full: "Finally, when he reached old age, he was ill for months on end and, seeing that he was about to die he fervidly returned to Catholicism, to the right path of the holy Christian faith, and confessed his sins, weeping and repenting ... When the King, too, arrived, for he would often visit him gladly, Leonardo sat up in bed as it was meet and proper and told the King about his illness and the sufferings he endured, admitting all the same how much he had offended God and people, as he had not worked in art as he ought to have done."

It is but natural to ask ourselves then: "How Leonardo ought to have painted?" Like Ghirlandaio, like Benozzo Gozzoli, or — let's say—like Botticelli? Perhaps so! Had he painted like them he would probably not have offended anybody: neither "God" nor people. He would have led the decent life of a common man and his death would have been a common man's death."

But Leonardo "worked in art as he ought not to have done!" This is something the artist knew quite well, something, however, which Vasari overlooked or did not understand when he described the episode of the end. Leonardo painted and drew with the élan of one aware he could not reach perfection. He never completed his works for even a simple contour would have broken their Unity. No doubt the implacable end appeared unjust to him, and the temptation — almost pagan — of noncircumscribed life, always flowing and infinite, appearead guilty.

It has often been said that Leonardo was basically obsessed by flight. Whether metaphorical or real, the obsession lends itself to amplification, for it was not the separation from the earth that persistently dominated him but the effort to deny discontinuity. The idea of motion *was congenial to him; he studied the human body as if it were a machine, a superb mechanism; he studied "the growth of the grass", the succession of geological strata in time; he drew tresses flowing, waters whirling and the endless spirals of birds in the sky. The static, even when self-evident, amazed him: "La luna, densa e grave, densa e grave, come sta la luna?" he wondered in a famous adage which, unfortunately, is untranslatable, in its perfect cadence.*

The fact that he lived like a pilgrim, endlessly wandering, was of course an accident external time enforced upon him. But how perfectly suited perpetual wandering was to his inner self! In fact there is no actual halt between the village of Vinci and the castle of Cloux. His notes, the dozens of sheets on which he jotted down his thoughts and remarks, tell of a second road he followed, a secret one. Sometimes distancing occurs, causing surprise, for the note in the corner of a sheet seems to us a distanced astonished remark: "O, Lionardo, Lionardo, mio quanto penate" (Oh, Leonardo, my Leonardo, how much you suffer!)

What is then the significance of the Work of Art for Leonardo? Could it be a break helping him to tarry for a while, a "bracketed" space, suspending the hurried pace of his pursuit in the calm pause of the image? Did he paint such a small number of pictures because he seldom allowed himself a respite along the uninterrupted road of intellectual experiments? Not very likely!

Leonardo changed the meaning and significance of the painting prior to him. The image is no longer a matter of "circumscribing", of "composition" and of "reception of light" as it used to be with Alberti. "Painting", says Leonardo, "is philosophy, because philosophy deals with movement . . ." The image, in the theory evolved by Alberti, made it possible to represent "the changes of place" (mutamenti di luogo), not the essence of movement. The "artificial" perspective implies a geometrization of time in its adaptation to the rational structure of space. Leonardo contrasts the "natural" perspective to the "artificial" one. The artist is no longer an artifex *but a* speculatore. *From an "intersection of the visual pyramid", the work of art becomes the space in which the world mirrors itself in man. The world without man is timeless space. So the work, as a human mirror of the world's space, becomes a "spatialization" of time. Leonardo expressed his ideas quite clearly: " . . . time, though one of the continuous qualities, does not fully come under the geometrical power able to divide it into figures and bodies of an infinite variety . . . ; it accords with them in a simple way, according to the first principles, i.e. the point and the line. If the conditions set apart for time are applied to the point, the latter must be regarded as a moment, while the line must be regarded as a more durable length of time. The same as the points constitute the beginning and end of the respective line, the moments are the origin and end of a certain period of time. However, if a line can be divided* ad infinitum, *the same can be done with a period of time."*

When we try again to examine Leonardo's work as a painter, we realize that, in real fact, the artist actually painted very much. It is true that his works are few in number, but each of them is a masterpiece, an experiment carried to its extreme limits, an experiment on the live core of reality. Leonardo's œuvre *carries great weight in the history of art.*

Nevertheless, his influence on the new painting of the Cinquecento *is not very important. Except for its stamp on the narrow circle of Milanese epigones and the decisive impulse it gave to Giorgione's landscape painting — and through him to the whole Venetian painting — his heritage in his time was limited. The whole importance of Leonardo's work comes out most obviously only when we examine the development of art in the 16th. century in its entirety. Its impact appears to be one of the phenomena which brought about directly the crisis of mannerism. It was not Leonardo's "manner" of painting that was to fertilize the artistic evolution of Italy, but his global experimenting with reality, the "universality" of his mind, the flawless development of his creative personality. Leonardo was to the most enthusiastic draftsman of his century, the artist who was best aware of the spectacle of colour, the most consummate artist in the arrangement of light, the most refined theoretician. He contemplated writing a "Treatise on Painting" which he did not complete — as he had not completed many of his projects — in which, however, he dealt with composition only incidentally. He did not give definitive solutions, he only showed the wealth of expressive means a painter can choose from. Painting is the thorough way in which creative man becomes a participant in all the realities surrounding him. Experimenting, meditation, option, these are the conditions of the artistic process. It follows that Leonardo first analysed a work of art in its genesis, which eventually also determines its structure.* "The painter must seek solitude and judge by himself what he sees, choosing what is more precious in everything he might see; the same as a mirror which changes into as many colours as those of the objects it reflects. And in so doing it would seem to be a second nature."

This plea makes us inevitably turn our thoughts to Leonardo's singular attitude to culture. One might suppose the artist was not aware of historical creation. Painting is "a second nature", the "artificial" perspective (a human, conventional, historical perspective) is replaced by the "natural" one. Moreover Leonardo considered himself an "uomo senza lettere", a man to whom the cultural treasure in books meant very little. His work almost in its entirety was the fruit of experimenting with reality seen from the angle of nature. Antiquity, archeology, classical mythology played a minor role in his work. The Christian Pantheon offered him only some "natural symbols". Beyond it there is the mysterious depth of nature, its implacable laws, the irresistible attractions of the idea of force and movement.

In his unquenchable curiosity, in his great thirst for truth, Leonardo appears to be an artist of cognizance. The air and the water, the fire and the earth are elements which reveal their essence in an immediate form. The identity of physical and aesthetic laws turns painting into a "second nature" and endows the painter with the intellective gifts of the philosopher.

We are bound to see in all this a dispute between Leonardo and the extreme refinement of Florentine culture around the year 1500. He rejects intellectual saturation, offering instead his refined naïveté, his astonished mind, his wide-awake curiosity, unfailingly bent on the essential phenomena of the world. Any attempt at circumscribing the tribute of his mind to Platonism or Aristotelianism must unavoidably be arrested before finding any solution. It seems that his motto as a thinker was "Back to Anaximander!", which does not mean at all a step back in the evolution of the philosophic conscience but a return to "natural" thinking, original and global.

The tradition of the Vincian mythography has conveyed so many contradictory images of the artist — from the dilletante of genius to the mysterious magus — that when we try to render the essence of his personality we come across an almost unreal creature never described so far and difficult to describe. Perhaps the fact that Leonardo was a man without bounds should not frighten us so much. Today we can approach his work only by removing the veil of any mystery or by rejecting it altogether. We might then stand a good chance of meeting the real Leonardo: so clear, so lucid, so human....

VICTOR IERONIM STOICHIȚĂ

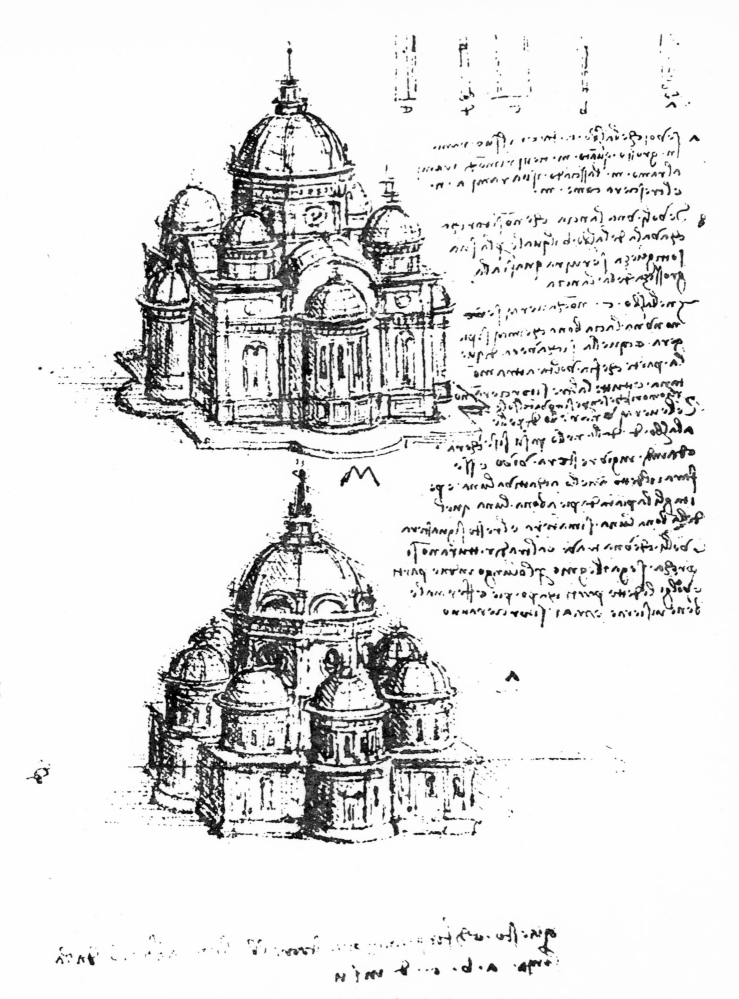

Domed churches on a central plan and study of proportions,
Codex B Institut de France, Paris

LEONARDO DA VINCI: ON PAINTING

On the first principle of the science of painting

The beginning of painting is to be found in the point; the line comes second; the surface comes in the third place; the fourth is the body covered by the surface.

The body is an equivalent of that which imitates the surface: painting does not go beyond the surface which shows any visible thing. (. . .)

On the second principle of painting

The second principle of painting is the shadow of the object by means of which it is represented. (. . .)

What the science of painting comprises

The science of painting comprises all the colours of surfaces and the aspect of all the bodies covered by colours; they appear to be nearer or farther as the distance diminishes or increases.

This science is the mother of perspective, i.e. of the visual lines.

Perspective is divided into three parts: the first refers only to the lines of bodies; the second tells us about the amount of colour that is lost with the increase of distance; and the third about the loss of any connection between bodies in the distance.

The first part — which deals only with the lines and the limits of bodies — is called drawing, that is the figuration of any body.

Another science derives from drawing and deals with light and shade; I mean to say clear and obscure (chiaroscuro), a science of great importance.

The science of astronomy has originated in the lines of the sight; it is nothing else but perspective through the lines of the sight and sections in the pyramid. (. . .)

The precepts of the painter

He who is not fond of all the things painting comprises will never be universal; thus, for instance, if he does not like landscapes, he finds them too simple to be studied and not profound enough, and as our Botticelli puts it, "a useless endeavour"; for when you strike a wall with a sponge dipped into colours, there is a spot on the wall, where a fine landscape may be figured.

It is true that the spots allow any kind of interpretation; some can descry in them heads of people, various living beings, battles, rocks, seas, clouds, forests and other such things. The same occurs when listening to pealing bells for you can imagine you listen to anything that crosses your mind.

Although such a spot of colour can make you imagine all sorts of things, it cannot teach you how to bring any to its completion. . .

The joy of the painter

The divine elements painting comprises cause the painter's mind to reflect the divine spirit itself; thus, before the eyes of the rising generations and of his own independent and powerful accord, the painter begins to create diverse living beings, plants, fruit, landscapes, plains, weathered rocks, dreadful and appalling places that make the viewer shudder; yet the same painter can also create delicate places, charming and pleasant to the eye, plains strewn with flowers in every colour swaying gently in the sweet blowing breeze, looking — as it were—in the direction of the racing wind; rivers cascading from the mountain tops, carrying along uprooted tree-trunks and boulders, roots and earth whirling in the foamy waters that carry along everything that might resist their fury.

The sea quarrels with the storms, competes with the winds, fights them, raising proud waves to the skies and collapsing under the blows of the wind which strikes at their base. And, riding atop one another they engulf everything, they tear and break and mix with the turbid foam, thus pouring forth their rabid wrath.

At times, defeated by the winds, the wave rushes out of the sea leaping over the tall promontories, higher than the cliffs, flooding the adjoining valleys and sending up into the air the spray driven by the angry storm, then falling in drops into the sea; some of it flows destructively from the top of the cliffs and carries along everything that dares resist its calamitous onslaught. Many a time the wave meets another wave on its way and, striking against it, rises to the sky filling the air with a dark foamy vapour; chased by the wind coming from the mainland the waves give birth to the dark clouds which fall a prey to the victorious wind. (. . .)

On the quality of the light necessary to paint objects in relief

Light, when too obviously crossed by shade does not enjoy the appreciation of painters; to avoid this difficulty — when you paint in plein-air — you should not let the sunlight fall directly on the figures, but you should imagine some fine mist or light passing through transparent clouds and floating between the figures and the sun.

The contours of the shade should not be too sharply outlined as compared to the illumined edges.

On the proportion of the limbs

The proportion of the limbs comprises two other parts, i.e. movement and quality. Apart from the proportions that correspond to the whole, quality implies that what is young should not be mixed with what is old, or what is fat with what is thin, or again what is lithe with what is clumsy, and above all not to give man the limbs of a woman.

Movement implies that the attitudes of old people should not betray the vivacity suitable to the young people nor should a young man have the attitudes of a little child, or a woman those of a man.

You should render the gestures that befit those who make them; it is the movement of the body that should bespeak a brave and stalwart man, the same as it is his slow, awkward movements that should bespeak a declining man, showing the decay of the body (. . .).

How to represent distant objects in painting

It is easy to see that the air which lies right above the ground is denser than the layers above it and the higher you rise, the less misty and the more transparent it becomes.

The lower part of the objects placed higher than and at a great distance from you is less visible because you can see it through a line that crosses the dense air stretching uninterruptedly over the ground.

The top of the heights we are mentioning reaches the eye through a line which, though starting from the place where you stand, in a dense atmosphere, ends high up, i.e. in a much lighter atmosphere than the one below.

That is why the farther off a line moves the lighter the atmosphere which it crosses becomes.

Painter, when you wish to represent mountains, you should show that, gradually, the foot of the mountain becomes lighter than the summit.

If you paint them lying far apart, paint the foot of the mountain in lighter tones and the higher they rise the clearer their real forms and colours. (. . .)

A skilful painter should paint two things: man and his mind.

The skilful painter must paint two main things, man and what is going on in his mind.

The former is easy, the latter is difficult, because you must render it by means of the gestures and movements of the body.

These he ought to learn them from many painters, who execute them better than any other. (. . .)

On the combination of colours in such a way as one should set off the other

If you wish a colour to enhance the beauty of the other, use the rule of the rainbow forming in the sky in the sunrays that pierce the vault of heaven, and which is also called the *iris*. Its colours are due to the movements in the raindrops, each drop changing its lines when falling to the ground in all the colours of the rainbow, as I am going to show in due time.

And now be careful, if you wish to render utter darkness, set it against pure white; you will likewise obtain dense obscurity with the help of a very light colour.

And what is pale will make the red colour next to it look brighter, which never happens when red is placed near lilac. We shall dwell at length on this rule later on.

There is also a second rule which does not purport to make colours much more beautiful than they really are, but which helps enhance their beauty by placing them side by side, as is the case with green when placed next to red or next to blue.

And here is another rule concerning unhappy combinations such as blue placed next to yellow, which turns white, or white placed next to other colours, about which I am going to speak in due course. (. . .)

On the perspective of colours

The illumination of the same colour placed at different distances and equal heights should be proportional to the distances separating it from the eye that sees it.

On the colours of shades

It often happens that shaded objects have not the same colour as the lighted parts, or that the shades are greenish while the lighted parts are reddish, though the object as a whole has one and the same colour. This happens when the light that floods the objects comes from the east, lighting by the very brightness of its colour; when coming from the west, the same light falls on another object, of a different colour from the first; through its reflected shafts the light rises again in the direction of the east, its rays touching that side of the object it struck first, breaking and stopping both its colour and brightness. I have often seen red lights on a white object with bluish shades. This occurs on the snow covering mountains, when the sun sets and the horizon is all aflame. (. . .)

On aerial perspective

There is another perspective too which I will call aerial; it helps us realize the changing distance of buildings of every kind standing all in a row, when seen through the various thickness of the layers of the atmosphere. Thus, for instance, we can see several buildings rising beyond a wall and above it as if they were the same size; but you, being a painter, wish to show them at a distance from one another. To achieve this it is necessary to show the atmosphere is dense. You know full well that when enveloped in such an atmosphere, owing to the thick layers of air separating the object from your eye, the objects situated at a greater distance, such as the mountains, look bluish and almost the same colour as the air when the sun is rising.

So you will paint the nearest building beyond the wall the colour it really is; the building farther on should be painted bluer and with blurred outlines; the building you want to paint farthest should be painted bluer still, while the one you wish to show it is five times more distant, make it five times bluer. This rule makes the buildings standing in a row look the same size and we will clearly see which of them is farthest and how much one is larger than the other.

On the change in the proportions of a body caused by the movement of the limbs in various attitudes.

The proportions of the body change every time man bends a limb more or less. The limbs grow larger or smaller in some part, according to the gestures they make, while they grow smaller or larger in the opposite part. (. . .)

On the general proportions of the body

It is the length of the body and not its breadth that should be taken into account. How wonderful and praiseworthy are the objects in the midst of nature and none of its achievements — no matter its kind — resembles one another.

That is why you, who change nature, mark the variety of its traits!

I am of opinion that you should avoid unsuitable things such as: too long legs, a too stocky body, narrow chests and too long arms; so take the measurements of the joints and mind the proportions nature uses in various ways, use them and change them in as many ways. . .

If you want to make your figures according to one pattern only, they will be all alike, which you can never see anywhere in nature.

On the description of the parts of the human body

The parts making up the profile of the nose are eight in number: (1) they are equally straight, concave or convex; (2) or they are not equally straight, concave or convex; (3) or they are straight in the upper part and concave in the lower part; (4) or they are straight in the upper part and convex in the lower part; (5) the upper parts are concave and the lower parts are straight; (6) the upper parts are concave and the

11

lower parts are convex; (7) or they are convex in the upper part and straight in the lower one; (8) or, lastly, when they are convex in the upper part, they are concave in the lower part.

The juncture of the nose with the eyebrows is of two kinds: concave or straight.

The forehead is of three kinds: straight, concave or convex. The straight foreheads are of two kinds: they are either bulging in the upper part or in the lower part; either straight in both upper and lower parts. (...)

On physiognomy and chiromancy

I will not dwell long on the fallacious theses of physiognomy and chiromancy. There is no truth in them, that is quite obvious, for such chimeras rely on no scientific basis.

I do not deny the fact that to a certain extent the features of a face reflect the disposition of people and their imperfections and character, yet the lines that separate the cheeks from the lips, the nostrils and the eye-sockets evince the joyous disposition of people who like to laugh. Those whose features are less marked are people particularly engrossed in thought.

Those with well-marked features, deeply lined, are brutal, irritable and foolish.

Those with vertical lines between their eyebrows are choleric while those with deeply lined foreheads are people who always complain either loudly or secretly.

Much could be said about other features too, especially about the palms of the hand.

It so happens that many die on the battlefield or are shipwrecked though their fates do not show in the palm of their hands which never resemble one another. (...)

On the movements of man and of other living beings

The movements of living beings are of two kinds: movement through shifting one's place and change of posture. Shifting implies that the creature moves from place to place. Change of posture is the movement which the creature makes all by itself, without changing its place. The movement through shifting is of three kinds: climbing, descending and walking on level ground. To these three I shall add another two which I should call walking straight and walking unsteadily, and one more, i.e. leaping. As to changes of posture they are infinite the same as the actions man often performs — and not without loss to him — are infinite in number. These movements are of three kinds: progress, simple attitude and the third is a combined movement of the former two.

Slowing down and hurrying should not be considered separate movements through shifting one's place, but only variants of these. The combined movements are numberless; we include here dancing, fencing, acrobatics, sowing, tilling, rowing. Yet rowing implies simple movements, attitudes, for the changes in his posture man makes when rowing do not combine with shifting his body but with the progressive movement of the boat. (...)

A human face cannot be praised unless it reflects the turmoil of the heart.

Those figures which through their attitudes do not reflect as much as possible the turmoil of the heart do not deserve any praise. (...)

On the painter's much sought for practice.

Painter, you who wish to prove your great skill, should know that if you do not start by becoming thoroughly familiar with the objects in nature, you will not achieve anything worthy of note. If you make a good start, your work will be quite remarkable and good; it will bring you fame and it will be of great use to you. (...)

Showing that the mirror is the master of painters

If you want to see whether your picture resembles the object painted after a model, take a looking-glass, look at the model in it, compare the object with your painting and try to be quite sure that the likeness is the most suitable.

Take the mirror as your master — I mean smooth-surfaced mirrors — for when reflected on their surface objects resemble paintings in many ways. Thus, painting shows the objects on a level surface, yet they look as if they were in relief, and the mirror does the same. Painting is based on the surface only and so is the mirror.

As to the parts that seem to be in relief or to have depth, you cannot feel them with your hands in a painting; the same happens with a mirror. The mirror and the painting create the likeness with the objects enveloped in light and shade; both seem to extend beyond their surface.

And if you know that through lines, light and shade, the mirror shows the objects have depth, and if there are among your colours more luminous or darker ones than the colours reflected in the mirror — of course only if you are able to combine them correctly — your painting too will seem to be an object from nature, seen in a large mirror as it were. (. . .)

On the elements of the opaque object

With an opaque object the part which is closer to the opaque object which casts its shade on it or to the source of light which illumines it will be more shaded or more lighted.

The surface of any opaque object takes on some of the colour of the object placed in front of it; but the farther the object the paler the colour and the nearer the object the brighter the colour.

The objects seen between light and shade will come out in bolder relief than those enveloped in light or in shade only.

On shade and its empire

The shade is projected on things due to the opaque objects which are placed in front of them and it is of two kinds: primary and derived.

On the two kinds of shade and the parts it is divided into.

There are two kinds of shade: simple and compound. The simple shade is created by a single source of light and by a single object. The compound shade is created by several lights falling on the same body, or by several lights falling on several bodies.

The simple shade is of two kinds: the primary and the derived one. The former is connected with the surface of the object which casts its shade on it; the latter, the derived shade, separates it from the shaded object, penetrates the air and, when coming against something that resists it, it stops and describes in the centre the outline of the object it started from; the same holds good for compound shades.

A derived shade always originates in a primary one.

The derived shades are arranged in straight lines.

The derived shade grows lighter the farther it is from its primary shade.

That shade will look darker which is surrounded by a brighter white colour. On the contrary, it will be less visible when set against a darker background. (. . .)

On the sunshine that gives light to the forest

When the sun casts light on the forest, the light and shade on the trees will be clearly delineated and will seem to come nearer, as their images are more familiar to you.

The part of the forest which is not bathed in sunshine will seem to be evenly dark, except for the thinner spots that are to be found between you and the sun, which will become clear on account of their transparency; for there are fewer trees lighted by the sun than by the light coming from the sky, and the light of the sky is stronger than the sun's and, in this case, a more important cause produces more important effects.

When the shade of the trees grows smaller, the forest does not seem to be thinner and it must have the same colour, and those which by nature have few branches and thin, such as the peach-tree, the plum-tree and other such trees, look as if they were smaller when the shade withdraws towards the middle of the tree, while the branches that are no longer in the shade seem to form a background of the same colour. (. . .)

On the shade of transparent leaves

The shade on transparent leaves seen from the back of the leaves is the same as the shade on the surface of the leaves. And it can be seen from below together with the lighted part, except for the sheen which cannot be seen.

When the green colour of a foliage lies behind another one, the objects and their transparency look stronger than with the leaves bathed in the limpid air.

If the sun casts light on the leaves placed between itself and the eye, without the eye looking at the sun, then the sheen and transparency of the leaves are very strong. It is very useful to represent some intertwined branches — for they are darker — against a lighted green and a little farther than the others.

Of the green foliage seen from below, it is the part closer to the eye that is darker, i.e. the part which is farther away from the lighted air above. (. . .)

On grass

Sometimes the grass grows in the heat of the sun, sometimes in the shade. If the viewer is placed in the shade, he will see the shaded grass projected against the light background of the grass illuminated by the sunshine; if the viewer is placed in the sunshine, he will see the lighted grass against the dark background of the grass.

On leaves

The lighter colour of leaves is due to its transparency when the leaves are placed between the source of light and the eye, or to some simple lightening of the air, or, finally, to some shining spots. The colour of a transparent leaf looks finer than it really is, while the colour of a leaf on which light falls is more natural. The shining spots on a leaf take on more of the colour of the air reflected by the surface of the leaf than of its natural colour.

The leaves whose surface is velvety do not shine. The shrubs, such as the vine for example, have very little shade on them, especially when the vine shoots are few and thin.

The blade of grass at its tapering end where the seed grows, will turn yellow sooner than at the base where it is attached to the stem. (. . .)

What is the real place of the skyline?

The skyline is situated at various distances from the eye, as we call a skyline the places where the sky meets the earth, seen in so many landscapes from the same perpendicular line hanging above the centre of the world, the higher the eye is. Indeed, when the eye is at the same height of a calm sea it can see the horizon about half a mile distant; but if the man rises to his feet and looks at the horizon, the latter has already receded about seven miles. Thus the higher you climb to see the horizon, the more distant the latter appears while the people standing on top of the mountains close to the sea shores can see the skyline very far in the distance. On the contrary, people walking on level ground, far from the sea shore, do not see the skyline placed at various distances, because the surface of the earth is not at the same distance from the centre of the world, as it cannot be, in every place, perfectly spherical as the surface of the sea is; that is why there are so many different distances between the eye and the skyline.

However, the skyline on the sphere of the sea will never rise higher than the tip of the feet of the man who looks at it standing on the spot where his feet meet the edge of the water and of the ground covered by water.

The horizon is often very close, especially for the man who stands on a mountain slope and sees the horizon beginning from the ridge. But when he turns to look at the sea, he will see that the horizon has receded far into the distance.

In Egypt too the horizon seen from the sea level is very distant. When turning to look at the Nile upstream, in the direction of Ethiopia, towards the boundless plains on both banks of the river, the horizon appears blurred, almost unrecognizable, because there are three thousand miles of flat land that rises slowly, with the waters of the river, and there is so much air interposing between the eye and the Ethiopian horizon that all the objects are coloured white, so that the horizon vanishes from view. (. . .)

On the real horizon

The real horizon can be found at the edge of the sphere of the sea, which I consider motionless, for such immobility reveals surfaces equidistant from the centre of the world, as we are going to prove in due course.

If the sky and the earth had been level surfaces, with a space of the same height between them, the horizon of the perspective would no doubt have appeared to be on a level with the eye of the viewer. But such spaces between parallel limits would necessarily stretch *ad infinitum*, seeming to meet and form one single line where the surface of the sky and the earth meet. And this line would certainly be on a level with the eye of the viewer. However, considering that the earth covers a smaller surface than the sky, as the surface covered by the sky descends to a height level with the eye and the skyline of the earth rises only up to the navel of the onlooker, it becomes obvious that the lines of the horizon do not meet in the same eye.

The sky and the earth do not divide their respective space into parallel lines or, better said, into equidistant planes, but into a convex space, when seen from below the sky, and into a concave one when seen from the earth, so that any place on the surface of the earth can become a point of the horizon.

LEONARDO AND HIS CENTURY

Leonardo was in the habit of going to his work very early in the morning — I saw him myself doing so; and he climbed the scaffolding, for *The Last Supper* was painted on the wall a little above the ground; so from sunrise to dusk he never laid aside his brushes and went on painting, forgetting about food and drink. Then it so happened that he did not touch his brushes for two, three or even four days running, and yet he would often sit for one or two hours at a stretch examining his work only; he would look at his figures and think and appraise them. I have often seen him towards noon when he suddenly felt like it, leaving *Corte Vecchia*, where he was working on that wonderful clay horse, and going straight to (Santa Maria delle) Grazie: he would climb the scaffolding and, taking the brush in his hand, he would add one or two touches to some figure, and then go away immediately.

MATTEO BANDELLO, 1497

. . . it is true that theory resides in the mind, but practice is based on the hand, and that is why the very skilful Leonardo da Vinci was never satisfied with what he was doing; he completed few of his works and he used to say that the cause was this: his hand could not match his intellect.

SEBASTIANO SERLIO, 1551

It is quite natural that the mighty heavens should often bestow rich gifts upon the human bodies; however, it also happens at times — unnaturally though — that beauty, gracefulness and virtue, all together and in plenty, are found in one and the same man, so that wherever he goes and whatever he might do his deed is so divine that it helps him excel all the other people and seems to be — as it really is — a gift from God and not something acquired through human skill.

This is what people saw in Leonardo da Vinci who, besides the beauty of his body which they never ceased praising, possessed an infinite grace that could be seen in all his deeds and so much virtue and so powerful, that all the difficult undertakings he imagined he achieved with great ease. He was endowed with great strength, skill and intelligence as well as with a wonderful and generous courage; his fame spread so widely that it was not only during his life time that he was appreciated and glorified, but also after his death, by his descendants who glorified him even more. Leonardo, the son of *ser* Piero da Vinci, was indeed a wonderful, sublime man; if he had not been engaged in so many pursuits and if he had not been absent-minded and unstable, he would have attained great eminence in scientific and literary knowledge. He started learning many things but, as soon as he started, he gave it up. (. . .) Nature had been so generous with him that in all his thoughts, feelings and actions he was so sublime that nobody could ever surpass his spontaneity, vividness, beauty, delicacy and grace.

It is obvious that Leonardo, endowed as he was with an uncommon gift of understanding art, started working on many projects but he completed none, for it seemed to him that, in all he undertook, his hand could not have reached the perfection of art; the more so as he continually thought out ever more subtle and wonderful things which his hands — no matter how deft — could never have created.

GIORGIO VASARI, 1568

Da Vinci's actions reveal a noble heart, a free and clear imagination, thorough knowledge, a powerful thought and busy activity; the beauty of the figures bespeaks mature wisdom; justice, reason, sound judgement are traits that help him distinguish right from wrong and ignorance; he is a partisan of glorious, lofty truth and of charity, the queen of all virtues.

(. . .) And yet he never completed any of his undertakings for he believed that true art was so lofty and difficult to achieve that he discovered mistakes in things that others considered marvelous indeed.

When distributing light, he was afraid of making it too strong and kept it for a more suitable place; and he tried to make darkness very dark so as to achieve contrast. Possessing such an art, he began to make such wonderful images and bodies that they resembled in every detail everything nature can create. In this field he was far above all the others, so that we can say that Leonardo's light is divine.

GIAN PAOLO LOMAZZO, 1590

LEONARDO
AND MODERN CRITICISM

Léonard da Vinci, miroir profond et sombre
Où des anges charmants, avec un doux souris
Tout chargé de mystère, apparaissent à l'ombre
Des glaciers et des pins qui ferment leur pays. . . *

CHARLES BAUDELAIRE
(Les Fleurs du Mal, 1857)

He was the first painter to have noticed the traces left by suffering on man's countenance. Before his time, painters were quite familiar with the body and character of man, but they could not render the fleeting change of the features caused by emotion. Leonardo studied this aspect of his art in every detail. He made innumerable studies; he left many violent and detailed caricatures which show how thoroughly he had studied the expressive effect achieved by diminishing or exaggerating every feature. His experiments on muscles, made with the help of a pencil, are very much like those Monsieur Duchenne (of Boulogne) carries on today with the help of electricity. It is only by isolating it and by exacerbating its function that you come to know the value of an organ. To understand this kind of discoveries, it is necessary to compare Leonardo's *Last Supper* with the same works by Giotto and Ghirlandaio. In Giotto's work the apostles are all motionless, sitting upright, with dignified countenances, yet devoid of any feeling. In Ghirlandaio's *Last Supper* — the one at San Marco Monastery in Florence — the characters are more varied: they are highly individualized, perfect portraits; however, the Saviour's words *"Verily I say unto you, one of you shall betray me,"* do not seem to rouse any feeling in them; they are not startled. Ghirlandaio found twelve Florentines and made them sit for his Last Supper; he drew their portraits and draped the cloth in noble folds over their bodies; that is all he did. On the contrary, with Leonardo, the attitudes and countenances of the twelve apostles reflect Christ's words. One of them seems to say: "Is that me, my Lord?" and he raises his hands in indignation to his breast. Others repeat Christ's words to one another and one can read suspicion and horror on their faces; another still is turning questioningly towards his neighbour, fearing he has not heard well. Finally, instead of withdrawing into the background as Giotto's puny, withered Judean does, Judas casts a piercing look at the apostles to see if they have grasped what Christ said and if there is any danger for him. Each separate face in the painting reveals a peculiar character and expresses distinct shades of emotion. Leonardo for the first time fixes on the canvas the accidental, the unforeseen, some fleeting moment in the development of human passions; his images are not only the representation of solemn, anatomically authentic personages; they reveal the ever changing emotions harboured in the heart and giving it life, which is the utmost progress and the extreme limit of nature's truth.

What is the character perfectly suited to such talent? There is always one for each painter, and the image he has chosen and rendered, willingly or not, is the best expression of his nature and taste. With Leonardo the image he paints over and over again is a delicate, sensitive being, almost feminine, of unparalleled distinction and gracefulness. (. . .)

Of all the old painters, Leonardo is the most modern; from the very beginning he carried naturalism to its limits; nobody grasped the complexity and delicacy of nature as he did; nobody was able to render it with such clever technique and complete devices. His scientific work was far in advance of his time; he devised methods, sensed truths and foresaw a system which we can hardly clear up today, he discovered in advance in the structure of the heads and bodies he painted, in their fine, mobile physiognomies, in the strange and morbid beauty of countenances, the complex, sublime feelings, so refined and charming, which the distinguished poets of our age have come to express; I want to say that he discovered the superiority and exigencies of a too delicate, excitable and contented human being, who needs nothing and considers that this is too little for him.

HIPPOLYTE TAINE, 1866

All that Giotto and Masaccio had attained in the rendering of tactile values, all that Fra Angelico or Filippo Lippi had achieved in expression, all that Pollaiuolo had accomplished in movement, or Verrocchio in light and shade, Leonardo, without the faintest trace of that tentativeness, that painfulness of effort which characterised his immediate forerunners, equalled

---

* Da Vinci, casting shadows over the mirrors deep, / From which young gentle angels are smiling in the night / Enveloped in their secrets, in the dark country, where / The pine-trees and the glaciers horizons wide close in. . .

or surpassed. Outside Velázquez, and perhaps, when at their best, Rembrandt and Degas, we shall seek in vain for tactile values so stimulating and so convincing as those of his "Monna Lisa"; outside Degas, we shall not find such supreme mastery over the art of movement as in the unfinished "Epiphany" in the Uffizi; and if Leonardo has been left far behind as a painter of light, no one has succeeded in conveying by means of light and shade a more penetrating feeling of mystery and awe than he in his "Virgin of the Rocks." Add to all this a feeling for beauty and significance that have scarcely ever been approached. Where again youth so poignantly attractive, manhood so potently virile, old age so dignified and possessed of the world's secrets! Who like Leonardo has depicted the mother's happiness in her child and the child's joy in being alive; who like Leonardo has portrayed the timidity, the newness to experience, the delicacy and refinement of maidenhood; or the enchantress intuitions, the inexhaustible fascination of the woman in her years of mastery? Look at his many sketches for Madonnas, look at his profile drawing of Isabella d'Este, or at the "*Belle Joconde*," and see whether elsewhere you find their equals. Leonardo is the one artist of whom it may be said with perfect literalness: Nothing that he touched but turned into a thing of eternal beauty. Whether it be the cross-section of a skull, the structure of a weed, or a study of muscles, he, with his feeling for line and for light and shade, forever transmuted it into life-communicating values; and all without intention, for most of these magical sketches were dashed off to illustrate purely scientific matter, which alone absorbed his mind at the moment. (. . .)

Painting, then, was to Leonardo so little of a preoccupation that we must regard it as merely a mode of expression used at moments by a man of universal genius, who recurred to it only when he had no more absorbing occupation, and only when it could express what nothing else could, the highest spiritual through the highest material significance. And great though his mastery over his craft, his feeling for significance was so much greater that it caused him to linger long over his pictures, labouring to render the significance he felt but which his hand could not reproduce, so that he rarely finished them. We thus have lost in quantity, but have we lost in quality? Could a mere painter, or even a mere artist, have seen and felt as Leonardo? We may well doubt. We are too apt to regard a universal genius as a number of ordinary brains somehow conjoined in one skull, and not always on the most neighbourly terms. We forget that genius means mental energy, and that a Leonardo, for the self-same reason that prevents his being merely a painter — the fact that it does not exhaust a hundredth part of his energy — will, when he does turn to painting, bring to bear a power of seeing, feeling, and rendering, as utterly above that of the ordinary painter as the "Monna Lisa" is above, let us say, Andrea del Sarto's "Portrait of his Wife." No, let us not join in the reproaches made to Leonardo for having painted so little; because he had much more to do than to paint, he has left all of us heirs to one or two of the supremest works of art ever created.

BERNHARD BERENSON, 1896

La Gioconda is, in the truest sense, Leonardo's masterpiece, the revealing instance of his mode of thought and work. Its suggestiveness, only the *Melancholia* of Dürer is comparable to it; and no crude symbolism disturbs the effect of its subdued and graceful mystery. We all know the face and hands of the figure, set in its marble chair, in that circle of fantastic rocks, as in some faint light under the sea. Perhaps of all ancient pictures time has chilled it least. (. . .)

The presence that rose thus so strangely beside the waters, is expressive of what in the ways of a thousand years men had come to desire. Hers is the head upon which all "the ends of the world are come," and the eyelids are a little weary. It is a beauty wrought out from within upon the flesh, the deposit, little cell by cell, of strange thought and fantastic reveries and exquisite passions. Set it for a moment beside one of those white Greek goddesses or beautiful women of antiquity, and how would they be troubled by this beauty, into which the soul with all its maladies has passed! All the thoughts and experience of the world have etched and moulded there, in that which they have of power to refine and make expressive the outward form, the animalism of Greece, the lust of Rome, the mysticism of the middle age with its spiritual ambition and imaginative loves, the return of the Pagan world, the sins of the Borgias. She is older than the rocks among which she sits; like the vampire, she has been dead many times, and learned the secrets of the grave; and has been a diver in deep seas, and keeps their fallen day upon her; and trafficked for strange webs with Eastern merchants; and as Leda, was the mother of Helen of Troy, and, as Saint Anne, the mother of Mary; and all this has been to her but as the sound of lyres and flutes, and lives only in the delicacy with which it has moulded the changing lineaments, and tinged the eyelids and the hands.

WALTER PATER, 1873

As compared to *La Gioconda*, *The Virgin and Child with St. Anne*, the other painting hanging in the Louvre, is less to the liking of the viewers. The colouring of the painting — which is probably not all by the hand of the artist — is altered; as a rule the quality of the drawing is less appreciated and sometimes hardly noticed by a modern eye. And yet, in Florence, the cartoon made for the painting roused such an admiration at the time (1501) that people went in pilgrimage to the Monastery dell'Annunziata where they could see Leonardo's new wonderful work. The subject must have been rather dry. Let us remember the rigid compositions, consisting of a group of three figures, in the works of previous masters: one figure seated in the lap of the other and all three facing the viewer. This time, however, an extremely lively group has been created from this arid composition, and the figures, formerly lifeless, have been invested with dynamic movement...

He resumes the same problems, already solved in *The Last Supper*. The composition is by far more interesting; a lot is expressed in a confined space; the movements of all the figures are contrasting, while the lines — diverging from one another — are directed in such a way as to make up a perfect shape.

We can easily notice that the figures are inscribed in an isosceles triangle. This is the fruit of lengthy searchings which can be detected in the earlier painting *The Virgin of the Rocks* where Leonardo tried to organize the composition in such a simple way as to form a geometrical figure. Still, this earlier work seems to be weak and confuse when compared to the cohesion and richness in *The Virgin with Child and St. Anne*. The fact that Leonardo tries to gather an even larger number of movements in a more and more confined space is no mere artifice: the power of expression is enhanced accordingly. The only difficult thing was to blur the clarity and upset the equilibrium of the representation itself. This was the trap into which his weaker imitators fell. Leonardo achieved a perfectly clear composition and the main motif — the Virgin Mary bending down — is of great beauty and of a moving expressive intensity. The cold affectation which easily submerged the painting of the Quattrocento was replaced by an unmatched power of expression. Let us carefully analyse each detail in succession, which lends relief to the lines of the shoulder and of the head. How pure they all are ! There is a valuable contrast in the unassuming attitude of Saint Anne, while in the lower part, the group is happily completed by the child who turns to look at the lamb...

The grass, the flowers, the small water pools that could be seen in the background of *The Virgin of the Rocks* have disappeared completely. The figures, full-size now, have become the essential element of the picture. However, an absolute proportion is less important in achieving a powerful expression than the relationship between the figures and space. They fill the surface much more than in earlier paintings or, to put it differently, the surface is smaller here when compared to the space reserved for the figures. This is the proportion which was to become typical of the Cinquecento.

HEINRICH WÖLFFLIN, 1899

This *symbolic* spirit owns the largest collection of forms, a treasury — always clear — of natural postures, a power — always imminent — which grows with the extension of its domain. A multitude of beings, a multitude of possible memories, the ability to distinguish in the world a vast number of different things which he combines in a great many ways — this is what makes up his spirit. He is the great master of faces, anatomies and machines. He knows what a smile consists of; he can place it on the front of a house, in the folds of a garden; he can ruffle and smooth down the filaments of water, the tongues of flames. When his hand describes various aspects of the attacks he himself combines, the trajectories of thousands of cannon bells open up in formidable bunches destroying the fortified crescent-shaped citadels and strongholds he has just built in every detail. He is very fond of battles, storms, deluges, as if the transformations of things were too soft and slow in their quiet progress. He managed to see them as a mechanical whole and to feel them in their apparent independence or in the life of their fragments, in a handful of sand flying wildly, in the restless sketch of each fighter in whom secret passion and pain are writhing. He can penetrate into the "timid" and "brusque" body of children, he is familiar with the measured gestures of old men and women, with the simplicity of a corpse. He knows the secret of imagining fantastic creatures whose existence becomes probable for there is such a perfect logic in the combination of their constitutive parts that it suggests the life and natural character of the whole. He makes a Christ, an angel, a monster, starting from what is familiar, from what can be found everywhere, and lends it a new meaning by means of the illusion and abstraction of painting which can present a single feature of things and suggest all the others. From the precipitations or slow movement simulated by land sliding or rocks falling; from the massive cubes to draperies falling in rich folds; from the smoke coiling above roofs to the distant arborescent shapes and the airy beech-trees silhouetted against the horizon; from fishes to birds; from the solar sparking of the sea to the thousands of tiny mirrors on the birch leaves; from the scales to the glittering shapes floating in the gulfs, from ears and hair-locks to the frozen coils of shells — all this is his province. He passes from the conch to the volute described by the waves, from the surface of the narrow ponds to the nervures that could hardly warm it, to simple repetitive motions, to fluid adders. He vivifies ! He gathers the water surrounding a swimmer into scarves, into bands that mould the effort of the muscles. The air behind a skylark on the wing he fixes in fluffy shades, in a froth of tiny bubbles, which these aerial routes must leave behind in their soaring flight along the azure paths of the air, through the crystal-like thickness of space.

He builds all edifices anew; he is tempted by all manners of combinig the most varied materials. He delights in all the things distributed in the dimensions of space: arches, frameworks, pot-bellied vaults; galleries and loggias in line; masses supported in the air by arches; bridges as if ricochetting; the intricate vegetation of trees losing themselves in an atmosphere that quenches their thirst; the structure of the migratory flights of birds whose triangles pointing to the south evince a rational combination of living beings.

He plays, he dares more and more, clearly transposing all his feelings into this universal language. The wealth of metaphorical resources at his disposal allows him to do so. The pleasure he feels when he keeps examining the contents of the most unimportant fragment, the tiniest glint of the world, revives his force and the cohesion of his being. His joy ends in festive decorations, in charming inventions, and when he wants to build a *flying man* he will see him rising in search of the snow capping the mountains and returning to the earth again to scatter it on the pavement of the town, steaming with the summer heat. The emotion he feels is reflected on the elated innocent faces puckered up in the shadow of a grimace, in the gesture of a silent god.

PAUL VALÉRY, 1919

Compelled as we all are in our century to narrow specialization, we find it difficult to understand the concept of "universal genius" in art or in any other field. While Leonardo, like all the thinkers of his age, took for granted that science is but one, that there is only one art and that many superior individuals can examine any problem only when related to all the rest, he believed, the same as they did, that such a programme could be possible. As his genius grew maturer, his art became more and more encyclopaedic, not only in his own field of activity, but — even more so — in the general relations with life and thinking. The clear-cut distinction we like to establish today between truth and beauty, science and art, could not exist in Da Vinci's thought. With a naïve yet sublime confidence in human nature, worthy of a Socrates or Confucius, he believed that activity and knowledge are one and the same thing for an artist, and also that it would have been possible for his contemporaries to apply this principle in the daily practice of art. The thesis that a painter should concern himself with everything is repeatedly dwelt upon in the *Treatise* (...).

All the works of Leonardo illustrate or defend these principles. More than any of his *confrères* he believed that art possesses a universal finality, that it is designed to establish a balance between the objective and subjective factors of vision and to bring together the technical and the representative expression, finally that art is able to transfigure the world of phenomena in its entirety through the accuracy of beauty.

Let us think of the other masters of the Renaissance, even Raphael and Michelangelo, who, of all the elements of artistic expression, evince a great interest in the human face only and concentrate their efforts on movement, pose, abstract manner and on the volumes of the human body; they seldom render the beauty of the animal or vegetable world for its own sake; how is it possible then not to admire Leonardo's versatility and sensibility to the impressions nature's "inferior" domains offer him? If, in this respect, the scientist helps the painter, it is not because of some limited purpose — empiricism or information, but rather because he seeks an ideal image of the world, permanent and universal.

In his drawings of flowers, he rivals with the greatest masters of nothern Europe in his fond study of details. He can pierce the secret of trees and flowers; he renders the organic growth, the articulation of the trunk and branches, of pedicels and leaves; his drawings make us feel the sap rising, the life and growth of plants even better than by observing nature itself.

OSWALD SIRÉN, 1928

The grotto in which *Saint Jerome* performs his terribly austere exercises is even stranger than the one in *The Virgin of the Rocks*. There is no trace whatever of vegetation and water here. In this world of stone where strange gleams of light circulate along the meanders of the grotto, everything seems to support the heavy and piercing petrification — internal and external as well — of the body and soul. One might believe that in order to release the spirit from the flesh the saint condemns it to suffer the most severe mortifications, that he wishes to rid it of tenderness, gentleness, humanity. The ideal he yearns after is to turn into stone, like all the objects surrounding him, like the lion too, with its harsh, bold contours resembling an animal carved in marble. And to make metamorphosis even more perfect, the saint strikes his breast with a stone, as though wishing it to penetrate under his skin and to replace the heart — the sensitive, throbbing organ — by an inert mass. The lacerated breast, the limbs carved as it were in grey limestone, the face purified of everything except the skin and bones, rigid and dry, as if made of wood, all reveal a prodigious metamorphosis. The lion, changed into an angular mass, Saint Jerome into a geological creature recalling a landscape of crests and gullies, the cliffs in the landscape where he appears, alive only through the life in his eyes, this extraordinary shape who almost furiously tries to identify itself with the stone, are the components of this painting which was never completed and throws such a strange light on the religious thinking of Leonardo.

MARCEL BRION, 1952

We cannot understand and appreciate correctly Leonardo's speculations on perspective if we do not take into account the fact that they illustrate the transition from a substantial to a phenomenal conception of the world, from a concrete anecdotical representation to a harmonious and mathematical figuration of the real, which is no longer considered to be what does exists but what can be perceived. As compared to the previous generations, the leap is surprising indeed, and any generation could wish to have such "efficient" men. The real significance of a discovery is not derived from its immediate application, but from the reversal it implies in the posing of problems. Leonardo's views on perspective are remarkable especially as they do not simply result from the methods he used in his workshop or from the application of some ideas he derived from some already explained intellectual systems. His speculations are connected with all his experiments in the field of science and mechanics. We would misunderstand his work if we imagined he simply discovered a more exact method than his predecessors in order to achieve an orthometric projection of material bodies against a two-dimensional plastic screen, function of an illusory immutable nature and of a no less immutable human eye. By introducing into his system the concept of movement and demonstrating the importance and autonomy of light and of the virtual image, Leonardo made of perspective something more than an empirical science. He made of it a part of science. (...)

Leonardo discovered the superior unity of a work of art in the wealth and harmonious integration of sensations. Hence an absolute opposition between the feeling of space and of time. On the one hand an imobile, rigid space, caught as it were in the beams of a projector, which has to generate the theatrical classical and baroque scene; on the other, a varied space, filled with a larger number of figures than the eye could discern at a first glance, so rich that only a correct intuition can produce the sensation of its immeasurable expansion, which is not rendered by the interplay of isolated scenes but by laws of proportion and effects of light. On the one hand, the figuration of time through historical episodes, a recollection of things already known, a projection of sensations into the rite, a renewal of facts and myths asserting their value and intelligibility; on the other hand the immediate grasping of simultaneousness, time viewed as a law and its representation, the same as its nature connected from now on with physical phenomena, subjected to the same mathematical laws as expansion is. Simultaneousness is time viewed as an activity of the spirit, not of memory. We must also add here a transfer of the concepts of joy and of creative power. Leonardo was to declare that you must love an object for no other reason than for its own sake and that the sun, which dominates the world, acts through force not through necessity. So the painter will play a double role. On the one hand, the things of the mind which have not been grasped are vain and breed only harmful truths, so that the supreme criterion of a work of art is mathematics; on the other hand, painting, whose system of representations includes the live spectacle of the world and not inert things, comprises all the forms of nature and is by far superior to literature whose words are not universal like forms. In the last analysis Leonardo considers painting a universal language which eliminates the accidental to give material form to the essential.

PIERRE FRANCASTEL, 1952

The Virgin of the Rocks is the last painting Leonardo made in the style of the Quattrocento and it is still pervaded by the charming gracefulness of this period. The masterly execution has not impaired at all the fresh expressiveness of the characters and the balance between natural beauty and ideal beauty has been preserved.

Idealization has lent the painting even more life. We can see it when comparing the head of the angel in the study for the same head made in silverprint, today at Torino. The drawing — one of the finest in the world, in my opinion, is almost perfect. The painting, more delicate, more fragile seems to be enveloped by the halo of irreality; this is again idealization, in the Gothic sense. The same can be said about the head of the Virgin in the painting hanging in the National Gallery, which, though not entirely by the hand of Leonardo da Vinci, is sure to have been sketched by him. When comparing these two heads, i.e. the delicate inspired beauty of one and the faint, waxen-like *chiaroscuro* of the other, we cannot help recalling that Leonardo's artistic theories carried him too far, at times, from what we consider to be the most significant element of his genius. When comparing the two Saint John, we come to the same conclusion. It is only the head of the angel in *The Virgin of the Rocks* in London that shows us that Leonardo, sacrificing spontaneity to the rules of art, was able to attain a new kind of classical perfection, although, in our opinion, this gain is not commensurate to the sacrifice.

A delightful naturalism of the details adds to this Gothic idealism. The hands, the legs, the hair are studied closely, with an eagerness seldom met before. Leonardo rendered their inner structure to perfection, but he took great pleasure in rendering the surfaces more especially the delicate skin, smooth or lined and dimpled, through a successful interplay of line and light, evincing a very sharp sense of observation. In like manner the plants and flowers are treated with a Gothic feeling of their linearity and recall the most delicately carved capitals of the 13th century. The Flemish painters, who like to sprinkle the foreground of their pictures with flowers, were never able to suggest such an organic growth and inner life. As for Leonardo's pupils who, following in his steps, painted plants in abundance, they never came to introduce them coherently into the composition.

Although we can find Leonardo's traces in the whole composition and in certain details of *The Virgin of the Rocks*, we should not forget that his initial intentions were utterly distorted. We cannot imagine what the tones on values were, or the general impression the original made, hidden as it is today beneath thick, successive layers of yellow varnish. In the darker places, a mixture of bitumen in the colours made the paint too dense and caused it to crack like dry mud, while all over the surface there are numerous traces of some earlier retouches. We must take into account all these elements before stating that, at that time, Leonardo's palette was dark, that he was a poor colourist. Even in its present condition we can see that *The Virgin of the Rocks* was once remarkably bright and pointed to a subtle sense of the reflexes; the use of bright colours is the trait that distinguishes Leonardo from his Milanese imitators.

KENNETH CLARK, 1952

The angel in *The Baptism of Christ*, a painting on which he worked jointly with Verrocchio in the latter's *bottega*, is an early evidence of his uncommon talent: besides a perfect command of all the technical means and of forms, it reveals an expressive force by far superior to the one displayed in the other figures of the group. The posture is free, unencumbered and, adopting here a principle that was to become permanent with Leonardo, the figure is built along several lines of movement, combined in a natural way, as if they were seen from different angles. The refined forms, the delicate modelling in soft shady tones, the imaginative arrangement of the folds and the organic clarity are particularly obvious when compared to the parts made by Verrocchio. Besides the angel, Leonardo also painted the landscape forming the background against which the two angels are set. This tiny part of nature offers a new world for the eye to see. In 1473, Leonardo drew a landscape whose configuration is the result of both his observation of nature and of his free imagination. The composition still retains some of the features of the traditional pattern: the rocks in the foreground, the precipice in the wide, distant plain... The novelty resides in the extreme sensitivity with which he regards nature; Leonardo discovers the atmosphere that envelops everything, he notes the transparency of the masses of air separating the viewer from the object and realizes that they help him perceive the objects in their most characteristic features. The luminosity or the moisture of the air influence the object, while the space is rendered by the succession of forms, accurately or dimly outlined, in the clear or misty distance. This is already a vision based on the physical perception of a phenomenon: the artist wishes to represent and make obvious the knowledge he acquired through direct contemplation. Leonardo was obliged to create his own means of expression in order to give shape, through drawing, to the object he perceived. In his early youth already, he expressed natural phenomena as such; in the drawing mentioned or in *The Baptism of Christ* he gives us a fragment of real nature. Both the drawing and the painting contain, *in nuce*, the condition of cosmic nature in as much as it is perceptible in its "similitude", i.e. in the image the way it is moulded and it appears to be.

LUDWIG H. HEYDENREICH, 1958

We know from the old copies made after the part executed by Leonardo that *The Battle of Anghiari* designed for the large audience hall of the Palazzo Vecchio was certainly an opportunity for the artist to display a monstrous tangle of bodies in fierce combat in which man's fury finds a perfect echo in the grimaces of the beasts. Leonardo's physiological studies show that the painter achieved a particular kind of effects which exceed by far Bertoldo's confused reliefs on the same theme.

Thus, the "grotesque heads" the artist scattered all over the pages of his sketch-books are not a scientific repertory of human teratology, nor are they "caricatures" meant to reveal the ridiculous traits of some unknown characters. They are an evidence of Leonardo's acceptance of the resources of ugliness which hurts him and which, besides the jokes of the "artifiziosa natura", are the jokes of his imagination which creates logically constructed monsters. The "divine character" of art can be demonstrated through the psychological efficiency of the horrible figures as well as of the delicate ones: the opposition between them includes in a peculiar manner, the entire development of the life of the soul. It would be difficult to understand the motif of the smile, as represented by Leonardo, if we considered it to be the loftiest quality, that is a symbol of the soul itself. On the ancient Greek marbles, as well as on certain figures belonging to Romanesque art, the smile is rendered by a simple curving of the lips signifying the soul in general. The Florentine sculptors belonging to the generation prior to Leonardo, and first of all Desiderio, had taken it over and introduced it into Florentine art not only as a sort of "fixed attribute" of the human face, but already as a more precise function of the face, possessing a definite "physiognomical" value. This moment of the expression implies fleeting nuances and their delicate mechanism. It is a kind of selfawareness and of inner distance. Insistence upon this definite trait is part of an original poetics and implies a particular style. It appeared around the year 1460 together with some other "psychological" curiosities of Tuscan art culture. According to his philosophy, the mouth and the eyes are the natural seat of the soul; the letter of Ficino to B. Bembo (1478) completes the allegorical description of beauty by recalling the irradiation of "the very graceful smile" which "represents the perfect joy virtue and the tranquil happiness fills us with."

The smile adds thus an essential element to the gentleness and insinuating languor of the faces; however, with Leonardo the smile acquires one more meaning. It is indeed the symbol of psychical reality and the manifestation of a sensitiveness bent upon. Yet this second aspect is enhanced by means of a minute analysis of the play of the muscles and of the creases round the eyes at the very moment when they start moving and not when the face is dilated in a broad smile of explicit joy and serenity; all this is a return to an archaic impenetrability. The smile is both an accident in man's organism and a symbolic datum. It is followed in its process by something else and thus becomes singular: the expressive quality is enduring, as much as possible, and the uncertain effect is underscored, so that irradiation is suspended and replaced by a vague impression of hesitation and expectation. In fact, the motif is taken from sculpture, with all the advantages of gradually melted shades, to which a peculiar charm, essential for the face, was added after Leonardo. The portraits of *Ginevra Benci* and *The Benois Madona* exaggerate reserve (the former), and cheerfulness (the latter). The veil of gentle resignation which was to spread over the face of Christ in *The Last Supper*, appears in the face of the Virgin in the *Adoration of the Magi* and especially in *The Virgin of the Rocks*. With *La Gioconda* — no matter if it is the portrait of Mona Lisa or not — the interplay of contrasted expressions is achieved by a very fine tonal envelopment bordering on the ambiguity Leonardo wanted to express;

it invites, yet makes useless, the innumerable literary commentaries that have always accompanied the dangerous masterpiece.

ANDRÉ CHASTEL, 1959

In February 1500, when passing through Mantua, Leonardo sketched a portrait in pastel of the famous Isabella d'Este. We learn from a letter Leonardo wrote one year later that he had made two copies of the sketch, offering one to the marquise and keeping the other for himself to use it as a cartoon for a painting he was to make later on. Fortunately, it is more than probable that one of the two copies was not destroyed and that the splendid cartoon hanging in the Louvre and showing the bust of a woman in profile is the very portrait of Isabella d'Este...

The head, turning to the right to show the face in profile, is placed on a bust which only partly follows the same direction; the hands are crossed; the hair gathered under a net, forms a mass around the cheeks and comes down to cover the nape; the dress is striped. Though the conditions in which the cartoon is preserved are far from satisfactory, the sketch still reveals the hand of an excellent draughtsman. A highly distinguished and beautiful woman, she looks straight ahead, in a simple natural way; there is almost no trace here of the enigmatic, impenetrable expression on the face of *Mona Lisa*. The artist faithfully recorded, no doubt, what his eyes saw and he did not even try to embody, like in *La Gioconda*, dreams cherished all through a lifetime. This sketch is much more than an effigy resembling the sitter, it is an excellent artistic work. The execution reveals a spontaneous conception and the whole cartoon was probably the result of one sitting only. Leonardo's never-failing deftness as a draughtsman was certainly of great help to him: he rendered, in rapidly traced lines, not only the contours but also the modelling of a face whose fine proportions had begun to be impaired by an excess of flesh. The flesh in its turn is chiselled to perfection; all the rest, such as the hair or the dress, is happily executed in a more spontaneous manner, which, however, is enhanced by a peculiar decorative quality.

after BERNHARD BERENSON, 1968

The Adoration of the Magi is an unfinished work that brings to an end the first Florentine period. This is the subject we meet most often in the Florentine painting of the *Quattrocento*; when taking it over in 1481—1482, Leonardo broke with an entire tradition starting from Lorenzo Monaco to the more recent interpretation of Botticelli (about 1477) who eliminated the sacred character of the representation changing it into the celebration of the family at the learned Court of the Medicis. Leonardo explicitly refers to this painting which exalts the religious piety of the Neo-Platonic circles, interpreting the theme in a symbolic key — neither historical nor mythical — and grouping the figures in a circle around the sacred apparition, instead of representing them in a procession. Then, further removed from Botticelli, he eliminated the hut too, and placed the Magi amid a crowd of restless people gesticulating and prostrating themselves before the Infant.

Botticelli, too, developed the theme in the sense of an *Epiphany*, or of a manifestation of the divine, rather than an adoration; but Leonardo would not take into account the social aspect of the theme (the homage of kings and scholars to God) but its philosophic core. As the basic concept of Neo-Platonic thought is inspiration or *furor*, he expounds and supports his own concept altogether different from the concept of *furor*.

Epiphany means *phenomenon*; therefore the divinity does not manifest itself in the abstract *idea* but in the phenomenon. The phenomenon surprises, moves, upsets, produces various reactions, sets the whole reality in motion: even the horses are rearing and shying in front of the divine apparition. The phenomenon can be seen and meditated upon: to the right a young man turns his back to the scene inviting people to come and look; to the left an old man bends his head in meditation. The phenomenon takes place in the midst of nature: the Virgin appears in a landscape reaching as far as the horizon and is seated on an elevation of the ground, near a tree with broken branches on the lower part of the trunk, while young shoots sprout at the top. Imposing constructions in ruins rise in the background; the branches fall and the tree of life blossoms forth when the phenomenon appears; the distant stage of history collapses while nature comes to life again. Both the figures in the near foreground and those in the distance are agitated by *furor*; but for those in the distance (those who belong to an already "ancient" history) *furor* is the fight of warriors on horseback, while for those in the foreground (touched as it were by the phenomenology of the divine) *furor* is the impetuous élan of feeling and of movements. It is therefore the phenomenon which brings together in a cyclic continuity, in an orbit moving perpetually, the world of nature and the world of man, the cosmic movements and feelings that agitate man.

The Virgin is not seated on a throne, she is a frail slightly bent figure drawn in a few curving lines. She is like a spindle, turning upon itself, and forms all around her a vortex, a whirling void. The mass of the figures is in a whirling motion which is arrested by the invisible barrier of this empty space: so the movement is not completed, as nothing of the reality of things is completed, everything is a clash of conflicting forces, the workings of a continuous change. There are no emphatic gestures but only acts that join in the whirling orbit (completely different from the Botticellian rhythm) of the movement of masses, of the space and of the cosmos. As if all those present, seized by a *furor* assuming different accents and movements in every separate personage, made up a single figure with many outstretched hands, many anxious pensive or astonished faces; as if an orbital movement of the mass, produced by the light coming from distant regions, were returning in the space, in a perpetual whirling movement. Indeed, there is no *phenomenon* but a number of compressed phenomena, of infinite causes and infinite effects. Leonardo's world is no longer *natura naturata* but *natura naturans*.

GIULIO CARLO ARGAN, 1961

In the drawings representing machines in the Madrid Codex I we can see a new manner of drawing coming into shape which, together with the architectural design, tries to perfect the methods of representing groundplans and elevations. The most typical example is folio no. 44 v. It is interesting to note that Leonardo seeks different angles from which to draw an elevation: in front, sideways, as if he wanted to successively present the points in an orthogonal projection, without optic distortions. The architectural drawing or *the industrial design* — as it is called in modern terms — seeks similar means of representation in the Renaissance too: in both domains, Leonardo participates in this process as an outstanding character and we can once again quote his words which demonstrate how deeply aware he was of the creative value of his drawing: *"Il disegno è di tanta eccellenza che non solo ricerca le opere di natura, ma infinite più che quella che fa natura."*

The characteristic features of the drawings illustrating the Madrid codices required the discourse to dwell on the typical aspects of Leonardo's drawing; however, this kind of discourse would not be complete if it overlooked the other aspects, the artistic ones proper, which are better known: the drawing of the face and of the landscape which Leonardo interpreted and rendered — as usual — in a highly original way as compared to the Florentine school, thus opening up new prospects for its development. There are no drawings representing human figures in the Madrid codices, but there are admirable examples of landscape drawings (...): mountain ridges, transparent, imponderable, yet so personal in the profile of the slopes and valleys that they can be recognized as his on the spot (...). To draw these mountains, Leonardo used light touches of red chalk, so that he managed to avoid harsh outlines and express the rich light of an enveloping atmosphere. He "seeks the masterpieces of nature" here, and we can but admire, besides the airy beauty of the drawing, the intelligence and receptiveness his written word reveals: "Do not imitate", he wrote, "but investigate." This remark refers to the drawings in the Codex too, seen from the angle of the man who searches, contemplates and experiments, under the sign of an extraordinary receptiveness and unity of mind which Leonardo evinced in everything he undertook.

ANNA MARIA BRIZIO, 1974

CHRONOLOGY
AND CONCORDANCES

1452   *April 15*, birth of Leonardo, illegitimate son of Piero di Antonio and of Catherine; in Vinci, near Empoli.

Lorenzo Ghiberti completes the "Gate of Paradise" for the Baptistery of Florence.

1452—1459 *Piero della Francesca paints* The Legend of the Holy Cross *in the choir of St. Francesco at Arezzo.*

1453   *July 17. The battle of Castillon, the last battle in "The Hundred Years' War". The English are driven away from the Continent (except from Calais).*

1455   *January 26. The Italian states conclude a pact in which they agree to maintain political equilibrium and secure peace in the Peninsula. The fact is confirmed by Pope Nicholas V who guarantees it (February 25).*

1457   *Death of Andrea del Castagno.*

1460   *Birth of Mathias Grünewald.*

1461   *Revocation of the Pragmatic Sanction of Bruges. Rapprochement between Louis XI of France and the Pope.*

1461—1483 *Reign of King Louis XI of France.*

1462   *Birth of Piero di Cosimo.*

1464,   *April 13. Francesco Sforza, Duke of Milan, occupies Genoa.*

c.1465 *Birth of Vittore Carpaccio.*

1466   *Death of Philip the Kind, Duke of Burgundy; Charles le Téméraire succeeds to the throne.*

1468   Death of Leonardo's grandfather Antonio di Piero di Guido da Vinci, at the age of 96. His son Piero (Leonardo's father), his second wife Francesca and "Leonardo, aged 17, the illegitimate son of the above-mentioned ser Piero", are mentioned in the will of the deceased.

1468—1469 *The frescoes in Palazzo Schifanoia, Ferrara.*

1469   Piero da Vinci and his brother Antonio rent a house in Florence, in *via* della Prestanza (today *via* dei Gondi).
Leonardo is probably apprenticed to Andrea del Verrocchio.

        Death of Filippo Lippi.

1471   *Birth of Albrecht Dürer.*

1472   Leonardo is enrolled in the fraternity of St. Luke (the Florentine painters' guild).

        Luciano Laurana works on the building site of the Palazzo Ducale, in Urbino.
Birth of Lucas Cranach the Elder.

1472—1476 The period of "free apprenticeship" with Verrocchio. Paints fragments from *The Baptism of Christ* (Uffizzi) and perhaps the *Annunciation* (one at the Uffizzi, the other at the Louvre), as well as *the Virgin with the Vase of Flowers* (Munich); *the Benois Madonna* (Leningrad) and other works lost today.

1473   *August 5.* The date inscribed by Leonardo on the drawing representing a landscape, today at the Uffizzi, is the artist's earlist dated work.

1474   *Andrea Mantegna completes the frescoes in* Camera degli Sposi, *in the Pallazzo Ducale (Mantua).*

1475   *Death of Paolo Ucello.*
        Birth of Michelangelo.

1477   *Charles le Téméraire is killed in Nancy.*

1478   *January 10.* Leonardo is commissioned to paint the great altar piece of San Bernardo Chapel in the Pallazzo Vecchio. On March 16, he receives an advance of 25 florins.

        April 26. The Pazzi's plot against the Medici brothers. Giuliano is killed, Lorenzo is wounded, but he manages to repress the movement.
August 7. Genoa regains its liberty.
Botticelli paints The Spring.
Birth of Giorgione.

1479   *January 25. The Turkish-Venetian peace treaty is signed in Istanbul, putting an end to the 1463—1479 war.*
September 8, Lodovico Sforza, nicknamed Il Moro, enters Milan and becomes the ruler of the duchy.

  December 29. Bernardi di Bandino Baroncelli, the murderer of Giuliano de Medici, is hanged in Florence, after having been caught in Istanbul. Leonardo draws the figure of a hanged man (Bonnat Museum, Bayonne).

  Death of Antonello da Messina.

1480   Leonardo works for Lorenzo de Medici in the garden of San Marco, perhaps as a sculptor and restorer (see Chastel). A document records the second marriage of ser Piero, Leonardo's father, to donna Margherita.
March. Is commissioned to paint the altarpiece of the main altar in The Church of San Donato a Scapeto. The artist promises to complete it in 30 months at most; it is *The Adoration of the Magi* at the Uffizzi.

  The "Council of the Seventy" through which Lorenzo de Medici exerts his despotic power, is set up in Florence.
Birth of Albrecht Altdorfer.
1481   *Birth of Baldassare Peruzzi.*
1481—1482 *Pietro Perugino paints* Christ Delivering the Keys to St. Peter, *in the Sistine at the Vatican.*

1482   Leonardo leaves for Milan without completing the *Adoration of the Magi* and the altarpiece for the chapel of San Bernardo (which will be first commissioned to Domenico Ghirlandaio, and then to Filippino Lippi, who was to complete it in 1485). Following a meeting with Lodovico il Moro, he probably writes the famous letter in which he describes his scientific merits, his qualifications as an engineer and only lastly his artistic competence.
1483,   *April 23.* The contract signed by Leonardo da Vinci and the Milanese painters Evangelista and Giovanni Ambrogio de Predis on the one hand, and by the *Confraternità della Concezione* on the other, for the execution of an altarpiece in the church of San Francesco Grande, Milan: it is probably the first time the future *Virgin of the Rocks* is mentioned.
It might be conjectured that at the same time Leonardo began the studies for the equestrian statue of Francesco Sforza.

  Birth of Raphael Sanzio.
1485   *Botticelli paints the* Birth of Venus.

  April 13. He seems to have received the commission for a madonna from Matthew Corvinus.

1485—1488 *The "Mad War" in France. The feudals led by Louis d'Orléans (the future Louis XII) fight against the Crown.*
1486   *Birth of Andrea del Sarto.*

1487—1488 Is paid various sums of money for the design of the dome of the Milan Cathedral.

1488   *Death of Andrea del Verrocchio.*
1489   *January — February.* Conceives the decoration for the Castello Sforzesco for the marriage of Gian Galeazzo to Isabella de Aragon. His notes (April 2, May 10 and 17) show that he contemplated writing "a book on the human figure."
July 22, Lodovico il Moro asks Lorenzo il Magnifico to send him "one or two masters" to help Leonardo complete the "bronze horse."

  Probable birth of Corregio.

1490   *January 13.* The preparations for the marriage of Gian Galeazzo Sforza to Isabella de Aragon are resumed (they had been interrupted on account of the death of Ippolita de Aragon, mother of the bride). Leonardo imagines a presentation of Paradise "with the seven planets rotating; the planets were impersonated by people."
April 23. One can read in Leonardo's notes: "...I have started working again on the horse."
June 21. Together with "a Science engineer" (Francesco di Giorgio Martini) he is in Pavia to help him with the construction of the Dome.

  Birth of Titian (probable date).
1490—1492 *Michelangelo carves his* Centauromachia.

1491   *July 22—24.* Leonardo writes in his notes: "Jacomo came to live with me in 1490 (1491) on St. Magdalene's day, at the age of 10." This is Gian Giacomo Caprotti da Oreno, alias Salai, the pupil of Leonardo.
Collaborates with Ambrogio de Predis and Boltraffio. Organizes a feast in honour of Lodovico il Moro's marriage to Beatrice d'Este. Designs the costumes for the procession

of the "Scythians" and the "Tartars" (Windsor) for the performance given in honour of Anna Sforza and of Alfonso d'Este.

1492 *Death of Piero della Francesca.*
1492–1503 *The pontificate of Alexander VI. Borgia.*

1493 Journeys to Lake Como, Valsassina, Valtellina and Val di Chiavenna.
On July 13, his mother Caterina comes to Milan to pay him a visit.

1493–1518 *Reign of Emperor Maximilian I.*

1494 Restoration work at Sforzesca, near Vigevano, the residence of the dukes of Milan. He probably begins the studies for *The Last Supper.*

Headed by the Dominican monk Girolamo Savonarola, the Florentine movement known as "i piagnoni" drives the Medici family away, and sets up a theocratic regime.
September 3. King Charles VIII. enters Italy, preceded by the duke of Orléans and by the French fleet which occupies Genoa. Beginning of the "Wars for Italy" (1494–1559).
Death of Domenico Ghirlandaio.
Birth of Pontormo.

1495 Starts working on *The Last Supper.* Designs a decoration for Castello Sforzesco. Death of Caterina (probable death). Is mentioned as one of the Duke's engineers. Works on projects to flood the moats surrounding the Duke's castle.

February 22. Charles VIII. enters Naples.
March 26. Emperor Maximilian offers Lodovico il Moro the Kingdom of Naples.
March 31. Setting up of the "Anti-French League," in Venice (it comprises Venice, Milan, Naples and the Papal State; the emperor and the King of Spain also participate in it).
July 6. The battle of Fornovo, between the League and France; the French army fights its way back to France.
October 9. The treaty of Vercelli between Charles VIII. and Lodovico il Moro is signed. The rights of the French over Milan are recognized.

1496 In a letter to Lodovico, Leonardo complains of the difficulties encountered while working on the "horse" and of the decoration for the Castello Sforzesco. Starts working on the portrait of Lucrezia Crivelli.

1497 Makes notes for allegorical compositions. In his *Novella 58* Matteo Bandello describes Leonardo's method of work on the fresco at Santa Maria delle Grazie.
July 21. Lodovico il Moro insists on Leonardo completing *The Last Supper.*

Savonarolla is excommunicated.
Death of Benozzo Gozzoli.
Dürer works on the Cycle of "The Great Passions."

1498 Fra Luca Pacioli dedicates to Lodovico il Moro the treatise *De divina proporzione* and eulogizes Leonardo who has completed *The Last Supper* and has drawn the illustrations of geometric bodies included in the treatise. Work at the Castello Sforzesco makes headway. The letter of Isabella d'Este (26 April) and Cecilia Gallerani's reply (28 April) regarding the portrait of the latter made by Leonardo *(The Lady with an Ermine?).* We learn from a document dated October 2 that Lodovico il Moro had made Leonardo a present of a vineyard near Santa Maria delle Grazie.

May 23. Savonarola is burnt at the stake in Florence.
Death of Antonio del Pollaiuolo.
1498–1499 *Michelangelo works on the Pietà in San Pietro.*
1499 *Lombardy is invaded by the French army of Louis XII. The Duke flees to Innsbruck.*

Leonardo leaves Milan accompanied by Fra Luca Pacioli. Passes through Mantua where he is received by Isabella d'Este, whose portrait he sketches twice, promising her to make her portrait. He probably goes on a short trip to Florence and Vinci.

February 9. The treaty of Angers; Louis XII., King of France, forms an alliance with Venice against the duke of Milan.

1500 *March.* Leonardo is in Venice. In August he is already in Florence.

February 5. Back to Milan, Lodovico il Moro is made prisoner by the French and taken to France.
November 11. The Treaty of Granada; Fernando the Catholic and Louis XII agree to conquer and divide the kingdom of Naples.

1501   In Florence, Leonardo draws the first cartoon for *The Virgin and Child with St. Anne* and paints a madonna (probably lost today) for Florimond Robertel, the secretary of King Louis XII.
September. Ercole I. d'Este tries to obtain the design for the *Horse* in Milan, which is deteriorating.

The French and the Spaniards occupy the kingdom of Naples.
1501—1504 *Michelangelo executes* David.

1502   Makes four precious vases made of rock crystal, japser and agathe for Isabella d'Este (is paid 950 ducats for them).
Leonardo is in the service of Cesare Borgia as an architect and engineer and follows him in the campaign, to Romagna.

June 20—21. Cesare Borgia, son of Pope Alexander, seizes power in the town of Urbino.
Bramante builds the Tempietto *of San Pietro in Montorio, in Rome.*
1501—1513 *The Pontificate of Julius II della Rovere.*

1503   *March 3*. Ambrogio de Predis addresses a complaint to the King of France to settle the dispute concerning *The Virgin of the Rocks*.
March-June. Leonardo lives in Florence and — according to Vasari — starts working on *La Gioconda* and *Leda*.
April. Leonardo is commissioned to paint a wall in the Pallazzo Vecchio, in Florence *(The Battle of Anghiari)*, competing with Michelangelo.
July 24—26. Goes to Pisa, which is besieged, in order to study how to divert the course of the Arno.
October 8. Joins again the Fraternity of the Florentine Painters.

December 29. The battle of Garigliano; the French troops are defeated by the Spaniards; Naples passes under Spanish rule.
Birth of Parmigianino.
Birth of Bronzino.

1504   *January 25*. Leonardo is invited to be a member of the committee which was to decide on the place where Michelangelo's *David* was to stand.
April 1. Leonardo begins to receive a monthly allowance of 15 gold florins for the cartoon of *the Battle of Anghiari*.
May. Isabella d'Este asks Leonardo to send her a painting representing *Christ Child* in exchange for the portrait he had not yet begun; she is willing to pay any price he names.
July. Leonardo makes the following note: "My father, ser Piero da Vinci, a notary at *the palazzo del podestà*, died on July 9, at 7 o'clock; he was eighty years of age; he left ten male children and two female.
Pomponio Gaurico quotes Leonardo *(in De statua)* as one of the most celebrated artists.

Michelangelo paints Tondo Doni.
Raphael executes the Marriage of the Virgin.

1505   Salai, Leonardo's pupil, offers to paint something for Isabella d'Este.
April 1. The duke of Ferrara wishes to buy a Bacchus painted by Leonardo; the work is in the possession of *ser* Pallavicino who had already promised it to the Cardinal of Rouen.
1506   *February*. In Milan, the heirs of Evangelista de Predis empower Ambrogio de Predis to represent them in the still open dispute the subject of which was *The Virgin of the Rocks*.
April 30. Ser Piero da Vinci's legacy is divided between his heirs; Leonardo, an illegitimate son, is excluded.
June. Leonardo goes to Milan for three months, by permission of the Florence Signoria. When in Milan, he draws preparatory sketches for the equestrian statue of Trivulzio.

Death of Andrea Mantegna.
Pope Julius II commissions Bramante to reconstruct the Basilica of San Pietro in Rome.

1507   Louis XII applies to the Florentine Signoria, wishing Leonardo to stay longer with him to complete several works. His request is granted.
July 26. Louis XII. intercedes with the Florentine Signoria to settle Leonardo's dispute with his stepbrothers concerning his father's legacy.

1508   Leonardo lives in Florence where (on March 22) he begins to write a book of notes on mathematics and physics. Works on *The Virgin and Child with St. Anne*.
September. He is again in Milan where he will stay with brief interruptions until 1513.
October 24. The dispute on *The Virgin of the Rocks* is settled through a lawsuit. Leonardo lives in his own house near Porta Orientale, subsidised by the King of France.

December 8. Pope Julius II. supports the setting up of the League of Cambrai *(France, the Empire, Spain, Florence) against Venice.*

Birth of Palladio.
1508—1512 *Michelangelo paints the ceiling of the Sistine Chapel.*

1509   Geological and hydrological studies in Lombardy.
        On April 28 he notes that he has solved the squaring of the curved angle.
        *May 24. The Battle of Agnadello; the Venetians are defeated by the French troops of the League;
        end of the expansion policy of the Venetians in the Peninsula.*
1509—1510 *Raphael paints* The School of Athens *in the Vatican Stanza della Segnatura.*

1510   Studies of anatomy together with Marc Antonio della Torre at the University of Pavia.
        In his notes he mentions two Madonnas, almost completed, of which one for the King.

        Death of Sandro Botticelli.
        Death of Giorgione.

1511   Journey to Florence for the legacy. In December he is again in Milan.

        Massimiliano, the son of Lodovico il Moro, invades the country.
1511   *Pope Julius II. sponsors the setting up of the Second League against France.*
        The Empire, Venice and Spain join the League.
        Birth of Georgio Vasari.
1512   *The Sforza family comes back to Milan.*
        Fall of the republic of Florence; the De Medici Family come into power again.
1513—1521 *The pontificate of Leo X. de Medici.*

1513   *September 24.* Leonardo goes to Rome again, accompanied by his retinue (Salai, Melzi, etc.).
        He lives at Belvedere, at the Vatican, under the protection of Giuliano' de Medici. Until
        1515 he is engaged in scientific studies, in mathematics more especially.
1514   Lives in Rome and travels to Parma, Bologna and Florence where, on July 17, he solves
        geometry problems. Contemplates writing a vast work on mathematics on curved surfaces.
        He begins studies for the reclamation of marshy ground.

        Death of Bramante.

1515   *January 9.* Leonardo mentions in his notebook Giuliano de Medici's departure from Rome
        and the death of Louis XII.

        Francis I starts his campaign in Italy.
        September 13—14. The battle of Marignano; the French troops conquer Milan again.
        Titian paints Sacred and Profane Love.

1516   *August.* Is engaged in establishing the dimensions of San Paolo Basilica in Rome.
        September. The Concordat between Francis I. and Pope Leo V.
        Death of Giovanni Bellini.
        Death of Hieronymus Bosch.

1517   Leaves Rome at the invitation of the French King, Francis I, and goes to the castle of
        Cloux, near Amboise, where he resides in May. Takes part in the preparations of the fête
        of Argenton (he builds a mechanical lion).
        October 10. Antonio de Beatis mentions the visit paid by the Cardinal of Aragon to Leonardo,
        and three works belonging to the artist: *the Portrait of a certain Florentine lady* (probably
        La Gioconda), *Saint John the Baptist*, and *The Virgin and Child with St. Anne*. He also notes
        that the old master was stricken by a paralysis of the right hand, which prevented him
        from painting (but we know that Leonardo was left handed).

        *October 31. Martin Luther posts on the door of the Church in Wittemberg the 95 theses against
        indulgences. Beginning of the Reform.*

1518   He is likely to have participated in the preparations for the fêtes at Amboise and Cloux
        in honour of Francis I, of the Dauphin and of Lorenzo de Medici. Studies irrigation works
        between Tours and Blois. In the last two years of his life the king granted him an allowance
        of 10,000 écus.

        Birth of Tintoretto.

1519   *April 23.* Leonardo makes his will.
        Dies on May 2. Was buried as he wished in the Church of St. Florentin in Amboise. His
        mortal remains vanished during the Huguenot revolts.

SELECTED BIBLIOGRAPHY*

J. P. RICHTER, *The Literary Works of Leonardo da Vinci*, 2nd edition London, 1970
LEONARDO DA VINCI, *Tutti gli scritti a cura di Augusto Marinoni, I, Scritti Letterari*, Milan, 1952.
LEONARDO DA VINCI, *Tratat despre pictură (Treatise on Painting)*, translated into Romanian by V. G. Paleolog, Bucharest, 1971.

Sources

B. BELLINCIONI, *Rime*, Milan, 1493.
A. BILLI, *Il libro*, ed. C. Frey, Berlin, 1892.
A. DE BEATIS, *Relazione del Viaggio del Cardinale Luigi d'Aragona* (1517—18), ed. E. Pastori, Freiburg, 1905
G. P. LOMAZZO, *Trattato dell'arte della Pittura*, Milan, 1584.
G. P. LOMAZZO, *Idea del Tempio della Pittura*, Milan, 1590.
FRA LUCA PACIOLI, *De divina Proportione*, Venice, 1509.

Monographs

C. BARONI, *Tutta la pittura di Leonardo*, Milan, (2nd ed., 1962)
W. VON BODE, *Studien über Leonardo*, Berlin, 1921.
H. BODMER, *Leonardo*, Stuttgart, 1931.
S. BOTTARI, *Leonardo*, Bergamo, 1942.
M. BRION, *Léonard de Vinci*, Paris, 1952.
G. CAROTTI, *Leonardo*, Milan, 1905 (2nd edition, Turin, 1921).
G. CASTELFRANCO, *Leonardo da Vinci*, Milan, 1952.
                     La pittura di Leonardo, Rome, 1956.
K. CLARK, *Leonardo da Vinci*, Cambridge, 1939 (2nd edition 1952).
A. DE RINALDIS, *Storia dell'Opera pittorica di Leonardo*, Bologna, 1926
L. GOLDSCHEIDER, *Leonardo da Vinci*, London, 1950.
L. H. HEYDENREICH, *Leonardo*, Berlin, 1943.
                     Leonardo da Vinci, Basel, 1954.
                     Leonardo da Vinci, in *Enciclopedia Universale dell'Arte*, Rome-Venice, 1958, vol. VIII.
E. HILDEBRANDT, *Leonardo da Vinci*, Berlin, 1927.
O. HOERTH, *Das Abendmahl des Leonardo*, Leipzig, 1907.
R. LANGTON-DOUGLAS, *Leonardo da Vinci*, Chicago, 1944.
E. McCURDY, *Leonardo da Vinci*, London, 1904 (2nd edition 1906)
E. MÖLLER, *Das Abendmahl des Lionardo*, Baden-Baden, 1952.
E. MÜNTZ, *Léonard da Vinci*, Paris, 1899.
C. PEDRETTI, *Leonardo. A Study in Chronology and Style*, London, 1973.
A. E. POPHAM, *Les dessins de Léonard*, Brussels, 1947.
M. POMILIO-A. OTTINO DELLA CHIESA, *Leonardo pittore*, Milan, 1967.
A. ROSENBERG, *Leonardo da Vinci*, Bielefeld, 1899.
A. SCHIAPPARELLI, *Leonardo ritrattista*, Milan, 1921.
J. SEGNAIRE, *Tout l'Oeuvre peint de Léonard*, Montrouge, 1950.
W. VON SEIDLITZ, *Leonardo da Vinci*, Berlin, 1909 (2nd edition, Vienna 1935).
O. SIRÉN, *Léonard de Vinci*, Paris-Brussels, 1928.
E. SOLMI, *Leonardo*, Florence, 1900 (2nd edition, 1922).
A. VENTURI, *Leonardo da Vinci pittore*, Bologna, 1920.
                     Storia dell'Arte Italiana, Vol. IX, 1, Milan, 1925.
                     Leonardo e la sua scuola, Novara, 1941.
Collective volumes: *Leonardo da Vinci. Saggi e ricerche*, Rome, 1954.
                     Leonardo da Vinci, Novara, 1956.
                     Leonardo's Legacy: an International Symposium, Berkley — Los Angeles, 1969.
                     Leonardo, a cura di L. Reti, Milan, 1974.

---

* It is impossible to collect the books, studies and articles devoted to Leonardo da Vinci in a bibliography, be it ever so brief. A selected bibliography can be found in *Raccolta Vinciana* (20 volumes, Milan, 1905—1964). Ettore Verga is the author of a *Bibliografia Vinciana* (2 volumes, Bologna, 1931) which, however, should be completed with the additions of L. H. Heydenreich in "Zeitschrift für bildende Kunst", 1935 and in "Zeitschrift für Kunstgeschichte", 1952. Other bibliographic supplements can be found in K. T. Steinitz's *Bibliographical Report of the Elmer Belt Library of Vinciana*, in "Das Münster" (1952) and in the *Enciclopedia Cattolica*, s-v., *Leonardo, Bibliografia Leonardesca*, Vol. 7, 1951.

Leonardo's Art Theory

E. PANOFSKY, *The Codex Huygens and Leonardo da Vinci's Art Theory*, London, 1940.
J. SCHLOSSER MAGNINO, *La letteratura artistica*, Florence, 1967.
L. VENTURI, *La critica e l'arte di Leonardo*, Bologna, 1919.

Drawings

B. BERENSON, *I disegni dei pittori fiorentini*, 3 volumes, Milan, 1968.
K. CLARK — C. Pedretti, *The drawings of Leonardo da Vinci*, 3 volumes, London, 1968—1969.

Leonardo the Philosopher

B. CROCE, *Leonardo filosofo* in "*Leonardo da Vinci. Conferenze fiorentine*", Milan, 1910.
P. DUHEM, *Études sur Léonard de Vinci*, Paris, 1913.
E. GARIN, *La filosofia di Leonardo*, in "Scientia", 1952.
K. JASPERS, *Leonardo als Philosoph*, Berne, 1953.
C. LUPORINI, *La mente di Leonardo*, Florence, 1953.

Leonardo — the Scholar

R. MARCOLONGO, *Leonardo da Vinci artista-scienziato*
Collective volumes: *Léonard de Vinci et l'expérience scientifique au seizième siècle*, Paris, 1953.

Leonardo in Romania

O. DRIMBA, *Leonardo da Vinci*, Bucharest, 1957.
TH. ENESCU, *Leonardo and the Waters*, in "Secolul XX", No. 10—11, 1975
I. FRUNZETTI, *Leonardo's Drawings, an Expression of the Spiritual Experience*, in "Analecta",
    I, 1943.
I. SABETAY, *Leonardo da Vinci*, Bucharest, 1967.

LIST OF ILLUSTRATIONS

1. The Baptism of Christ, *detail*

2. ANDREA DEL VERROCHIO and
   LEONARDO DA VINCI, The Baptism of Christ
3. The Baptism of Christ, *detail*

8. The Annunciation

9. Portrait of a Woman (Ginevra Benci?)

11. Virgin and Child (The Virgin with the Vase of Flowers)

12. Virgin and Child, *detail*

13. The Adoration of the Magi, *detail*

14. The Adoration of the Magi

17. The Virgin of the Rocks (attributed)
18. The Virgin of the Rocks (London), *detail*

19. The Virgin of the Rocks (Paris), *detail*
20. The Virgin of the Rocks (Paris)

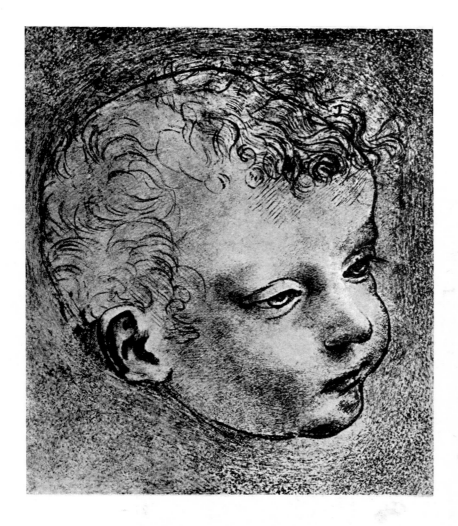

21. Head of a Child *(Study for* The Virgin of the Rocks)
22. *Study of Figure for* The Last Supper
23. Head of an Angel *(Study for* The Virgin of the Rocks)

24. Virgin and Child (Madonna Litta) — attributed

25. St. Jerome

29. Christ *(Study for* The Last Supper)
30. The Last Supper, *detail*

34. Portrait of a Young Woman

38. Portrait of a Musician (Franchino Gaffurio?) — attributed

40. The Lady with an Ermine (Cecilia Gallerani?) — attributed

43. The Virgin and Child with St. Anne and the Infant St. John

44. Mona Lisa (La Gioconda), *detail*

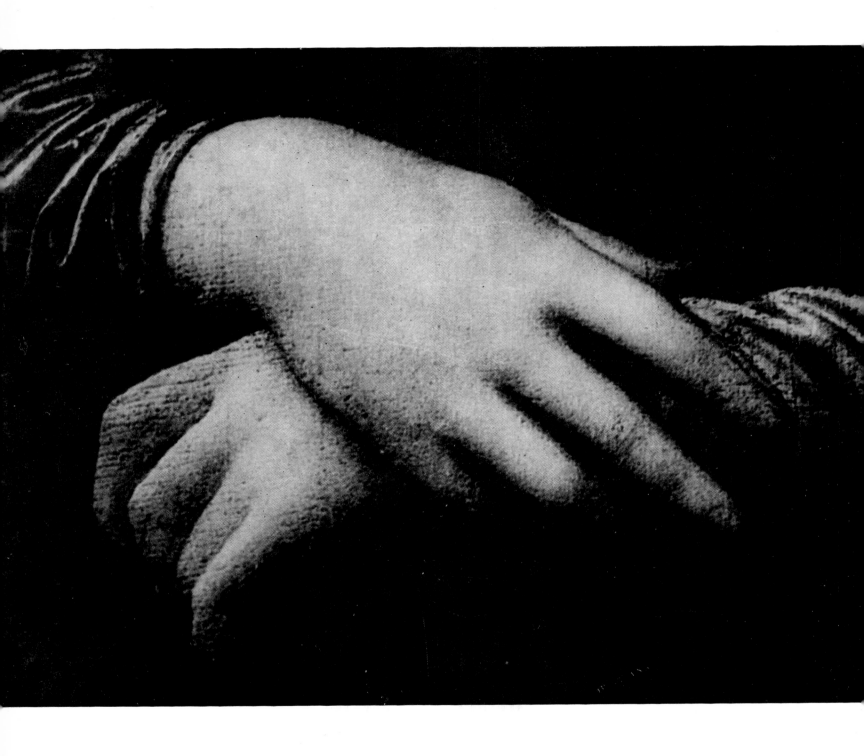

45. Mona Lisa (La Gioconda)

50. The Virgin and Child with St. Anne

51. The Courtyard of the Arsenal
52—53. *Studies for* The Battle of Anghiari

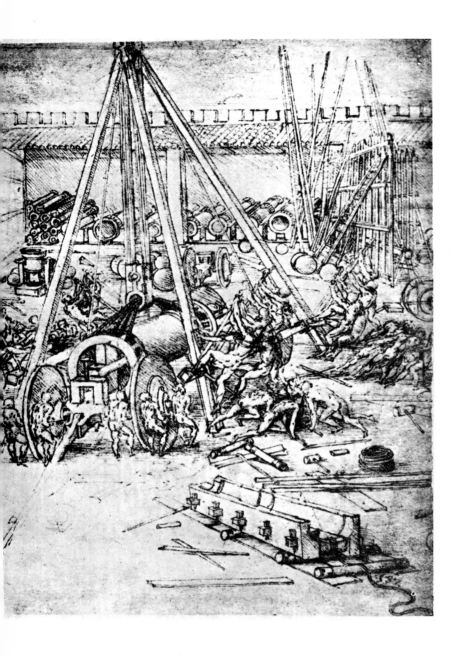

54. PIETER PAUL RUBENS
    Copy after The Battle of Anghiari
55. *Study for* The Battle of Anghiari, *detail*

56. Bacchus (attributed)
57 St. John the Baptist

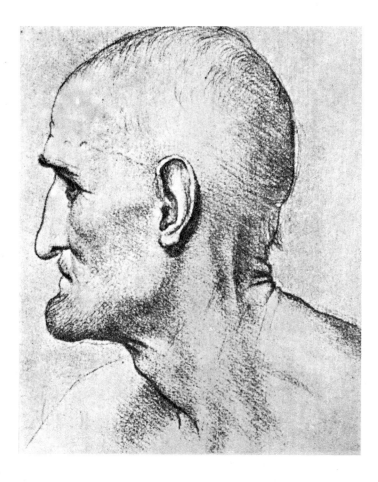

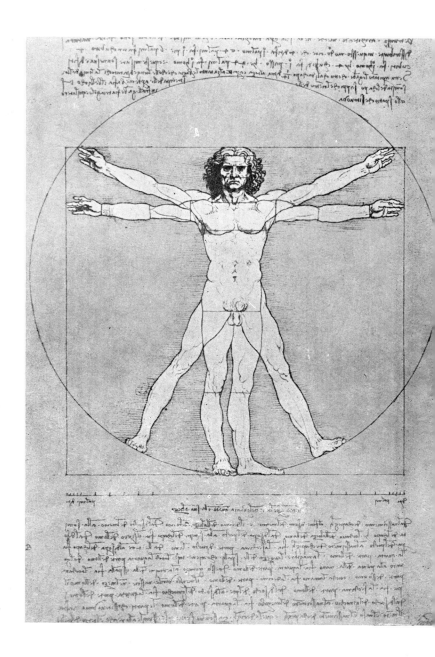

61. Aerial View of the Province of Arezzo

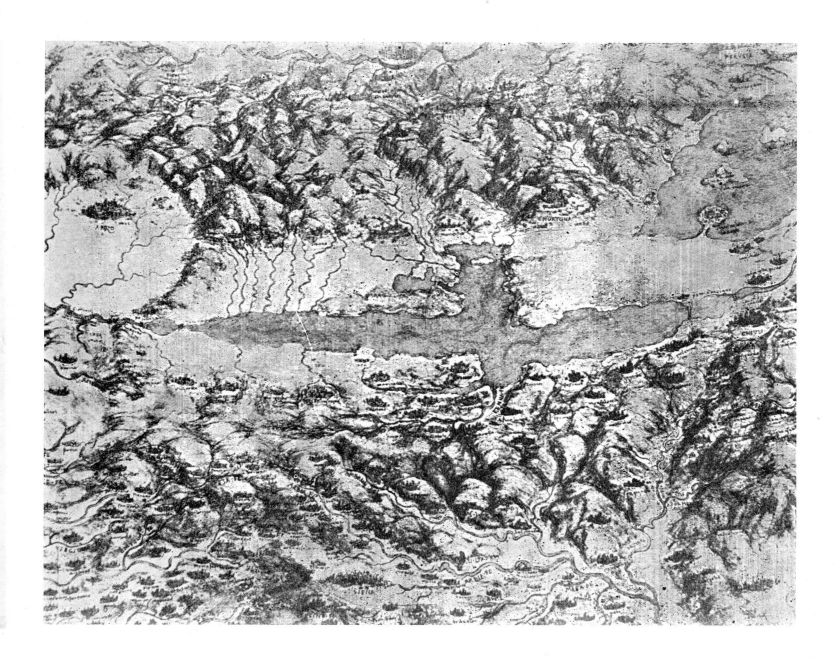

62. The Condottiere
63. Self-Portrait (?)

MERIDIANE PUBLISHING HOUSE
BUCHAREST

PRINTED IN ROMANIA